THE SPACE TRAVELLER'S GUIDE

THE SUN AND STARS

GILES SPARROW

WAYLAND

First published in Great Britain in 2025
by Wayland
Copyright © Hodder and Stoughton, 2025
(Text has appeared in *Space Travel Guides: The Sun and Stars*
(Franklin Watts, 2011), but has been updated for this edition.)

Editor: Grace Glendinning
Packager: Smart Design Studio
Illustrators: David Shephard and Joanna Davala

Picture credits:
P28 top left: NASA, ESA, and The Hubble Heritage Team (STScI/AURA)
P28 top right: E.J. Schreier (STScI), and NASA
P28 bottom: Wikimedia Commons/Simon Tyran (CC BY-SA 4.0)
P29 top left: NASA
P29 top right: NASA/CXC/Eureka Scientific/M.Roberts et al.
P29 bottom: NASA

HB ISBN: 978 1 5263 2820 5
PB ISBN: 978 1 5263 2822 9
EBOOK ISBN: 978 1 5263 2821 2

Printed and bound in China

FSC
www.fsc.org

MIX
Paper | Supporting
responsible forestry
FSC® C104740

Wayland, an imprint of
Hachette Children's Group
Part of Hodder and Stoughton
Carmelite House
50 Victoria Embankment
London EC4Y 0DZ

An Hachette UK Company
www.hachette.co.uk
www.hachettechildrens.co.uk

The authorised representative in the EEA is Hachette Ireland,
8 Castlecourt Centre, Dublin 15, D15 XTP3, Ireland (email: info@hbgi.ie)

CONTENTS

TWINKLE, TWINKLE

IN THIS BOOK, WE'RE LEAVING EARTH TO TRAVEL PAST THE SUN, ACROSS OUR GALAXY AND FINALLY OUT INTO THE UNIVERSE, LOOKING AT THE COUNTLESS STARS AND OTHER OBJECTS THAT FILL THE COSMOS.

WHAT IS A STAR?

Stars are dense balls of gas that shine because of nuclear reactions in their cores (see page 10) – they create their own energy and light.

Stars come in a huge range of sizes. Some are barely the size of Jupiter, while others are so big they would engulf Jupiter's entire orbit around the Sun.

Stars' brightness also varies – from brilliant giants 100,000 times brighter than the Sun, to weak dwarf stars 100,000 times fainter.

A star's colour is determined by its surface temperature, running from cool red and orange to scorching blue and violet.

THE SOLAR SYSTEM

This book journeys first to the Sun – our nearest star – and then through a whole range of objects that reveal the life story of a typical star.

Finally, we'll take a look at our 'star city', or galaxy, and venture millions of light years (one light year is about 9.5 million million km) into the Universe to look at the different types of galaxy that are out there.

NEED TO KNOW

The stars closest to our solar system reveal some of the huge variety of stars in the Universe.

THE SUN: Our star is yellow-white, with a pretty average size and temperature.

PROXIMA CENTAURI: This feeble red dwarf star is so faint you can only see its reddish light through a telescope, even though it's the next closest star to Earth – only 4.2 light years away!

RIGEL: With a mass about 17 times that of the Sun, this blue supergiant is the sixth brightest star in our sky. It is located in the constellation of Orion.

ANTARES: A massive red supergiant star, Antares is 800 times wider than the Sun.

SIRIUS A: The brightest star in our sky lies 8.6 light years from Earth. It is brilliant white and is twice the mass of the Sun.

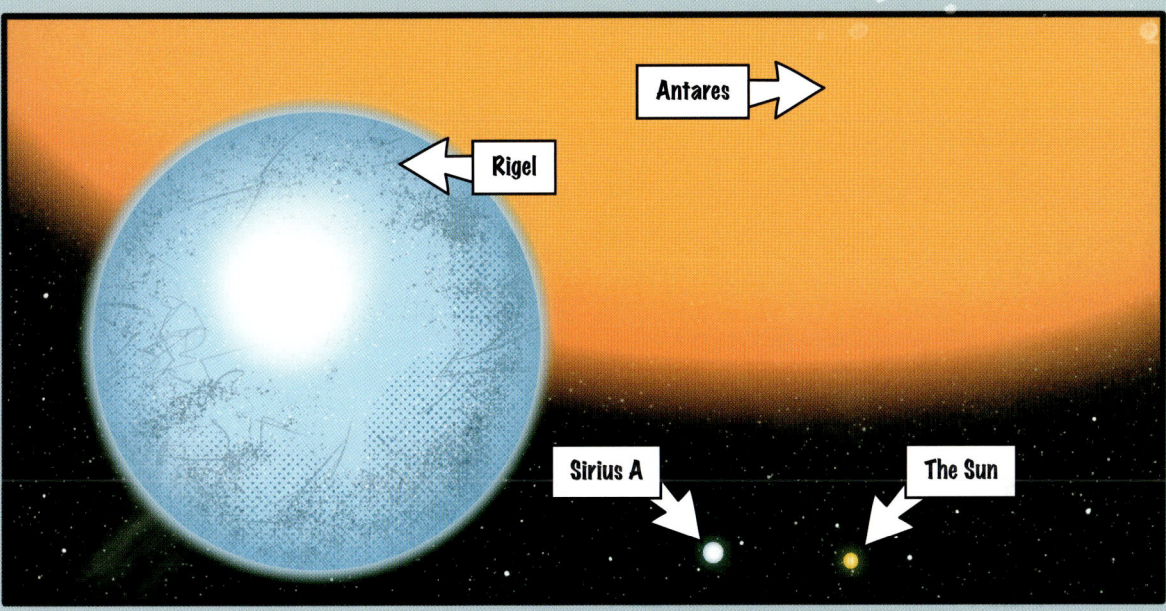

Antares

Rigel

Sirius A

The Sun

TRAVELLER'S TIPS - A SAFE WAY TO STUDY THE SUN

If you only take one piece of advice in this book, make sure it's this: NEVER try to look at the Sun directly. Its light is brilliant enough to damage your eyesight permanently.

In the early days of astronomy, many stargazers damaged their eyesight before learning the safe way to study the Sun – by projecting its image onto a surface. To do this, point a telescope at the Sun, but do not look through it. Hold a piece of card behind the eyepiece so that the Sun's disc appears on it.

THE SUN

THE NEAREST STAR OF ALL IS JUST 150 MILLION KM FROM EARTH – THE SUN. THIS HUGE BALL OF EXPLODING GAS, MEASURING 1.4 MILLION KM ACROSS, PRODUCES A BLAZE OF HEAT AND LIGHT THAT ENABLES LIFE TO SURVIVE ON OUR PLANET. IT'S ESSENTIAL TO US, BUT THE SUN IS REALLY JUST AN AVERAGE STAR.

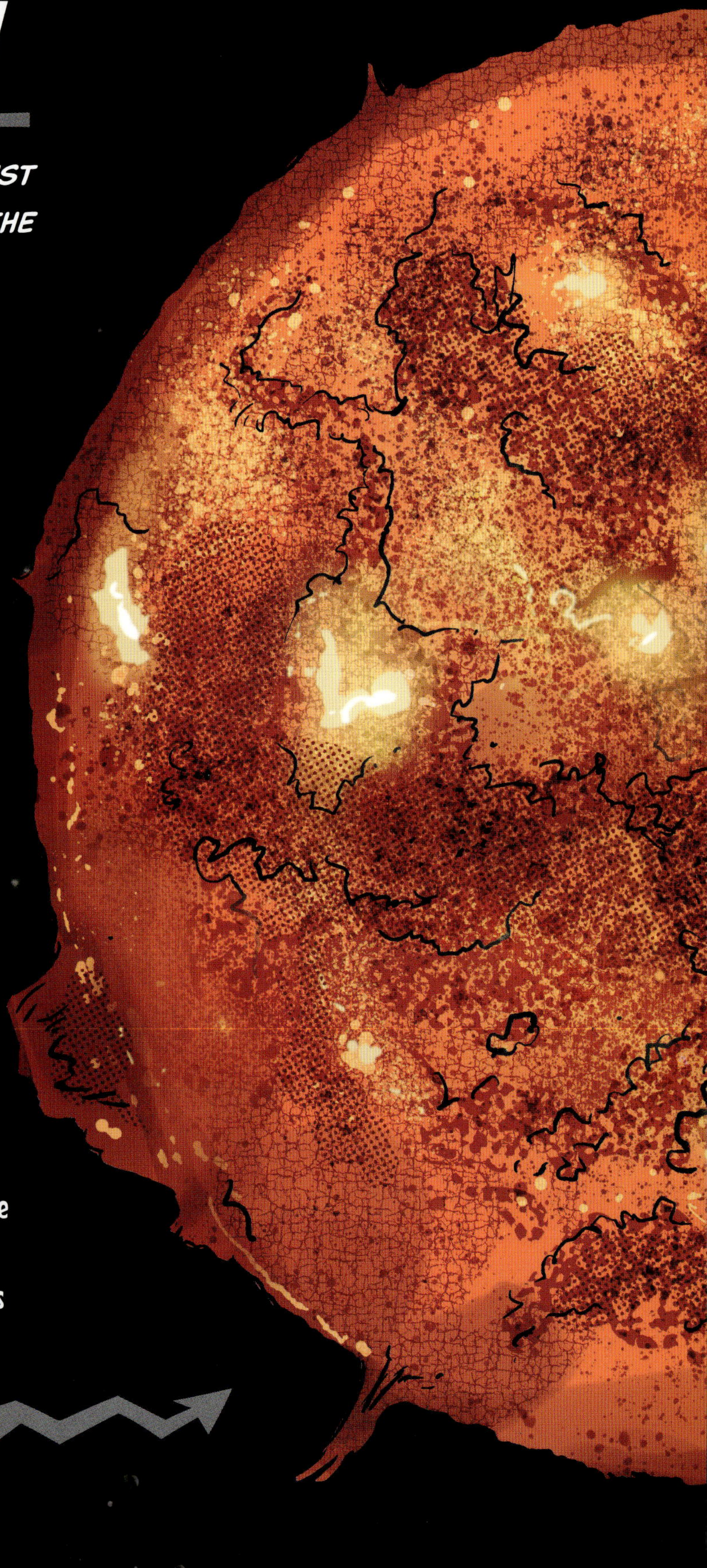

BLAZING FIREBALL

The Sun is too bright to look at directly, but special filters can help to show off some of its surface features. The Sun has a surprisingly 'sharp' edge – a layer called the photosphere.

Light is created at the centre of the Sun, but the interior is 'foggy' and stops the light getting out. The photosphere layer – with a temperature of around 5,500°C – is where the 'fog' lifts and light escapes, allowing the Sun's surface features to become visible.

The Sun has a huge influence over the space around it. It pumps out more energy in a second than all of Earth's power stations would produce in hundreds of thousands of years. This energy spreads out as heat and light, keeping the inner solar system (out to around the orbit of Mars) fairly warm.

The Sun's gravity is felt across a much broader region of space than its energy. It traps planets and smaller objects in orbit up to about one light year away.

Huge jets of hydrogen gas shoot out at regular intervals from the Sun's surface.

THE SOLAR WIND

Light is not the only thing escaping from the solar surface. A blizzard of tiny electrically charged particles constantly blows away from the photosphere and out across the solar system. Be careful! Some of its particles travel so fast that they will pass straight through an unshielded spaceship – and a human.

Planets with strong magnetic fields, such as Earth and Jupiter, trap solar wind particles. The fields funnel the particles towards the planet's north and south poles.

Solar wind particles collide with Earth's magnetic field above the North Pole, creating swirling patterns of light called aurorae.

FLARES AND SPOTS

FROM A DISTANCE, THE SUN MIGHT LOOK LIKE A FEATURELESS DISC, BUT UP CLOSE THERE'S A LOT GOING ON. LOOK OUT FOR HUGE ARCS OF GAS, OR FLARES, LOOPING OUT FROM THE SURFACE. YOU'LL ALSO SEE DARK AREAS CALLED SUNSPOTS, WHICH CAN BE AS BIG AS A PLANET!

PROMINENCES AND SOLAR FLARES

Prominences are ever-changing loops of pinkish gas that hang near the Sun's surface. They are visible through special filters or when the Sun's bright disc is blocked out – for example, when Earth's Moon eclipses it (see page 29).

Solar flares are huge prominences that suddenly burst apart, flinging great clouds of gassy material out into the solar system at supersonic speeds.

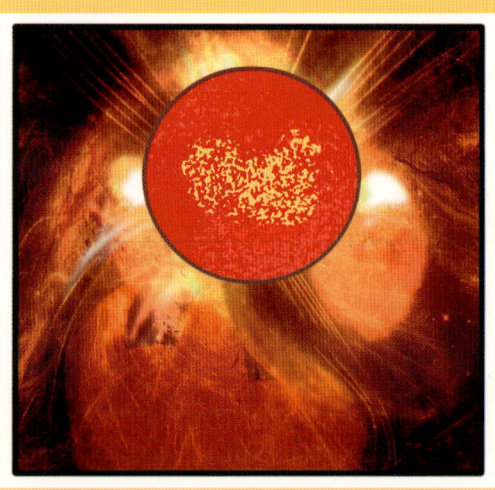

Sunspots form where loops of magnetism cool the photosphere. Flares often happen above them.

SUNSPOTS

Sunspots are patches on the Sun's surface that look dark, as they are much cooler (around 3,500°C) than the surrounding area. Up close they look like a pattern of iron filings disturbed by a magnet. This is because they are found at the end of huge loops of magnetism.

Nearly all of the Sun's core is made from hydrogen gas, the lightest element of all. The extreme pressure in the core forces the hydrogen atoms together to form the next lightest element, helium.

This process is called nuclear fusion, and it creates enormous amounts of energy that heats the core to 15 million °C.

NOT TO MISS

SPICULES: Towering pillars of flame, as tall as Earth is wide, that carry energy from the photosphere into the upper reaches of the Sun's atmosphere.

CHROMOSPHERE: This cool region just above the photosphere forms a layer where prominences appear.

TRANSITION REGION: A mysterious layer above the chromosphere where the Sun's atmosphere is suddenly heated from a few thousand °C to more than 1 million °C.

CORONA: The Sun's outer atmosphere, which extends for millions of kilometres into space.

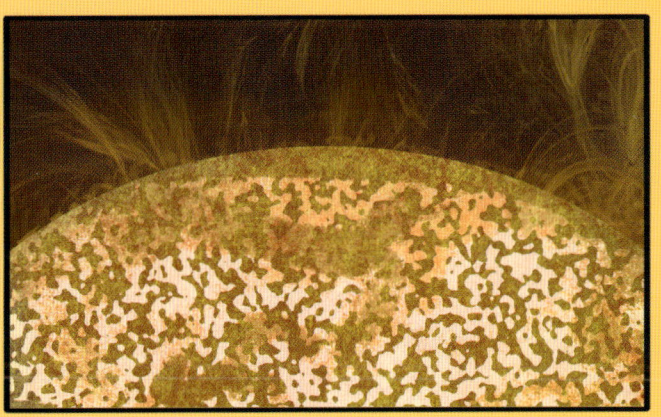

The Sun's spotty texture is called granulation. A typical bubble, or granule, measures 1,000 km in diameter.

JOURNEY TO THE TOP

Nuclear fusion energy forces its way out of the Sun's core, but it has a long way to go to reach the surface. For tens of thousands of years, it bounces around in the solar interior.

Eventually, it reaches a point where the energy is carried upwards over the course of a few days in huge bubbles, or granules.

Near the Sun's surface, the energy is released from the top of the bubbles, escaping into space as heat and light.

THE BIRTH OF A STAR

STARS ARE BORN IN HUGE CLOUDS OF DUST AND GAS, WHICH ARE MANY LIGHT YEARS ACROSS, CALLED NEBULAE. ONCE THE PROCESS OF STAR CREATION STARTS, A NEBULA CAN LIGHT UP IN A SPECTACULAR RANGE OF COLOURS.

SLOW COLLAPSE

Star birth takes thousands of years. It starts when a small clump of gas and dust within a larger nebula gets compressed until it is dense enough to pull in material around it by gravity.

More and more gas gets packed into a smaller space and grows hotter and hotter. Eventually, the heart of the collapsing cloud is so hot and dense that nuclear reactions begin, and a star is born.

This is how our Sun was born, about five billion years ago.

The Orion Nebula is one of the brightest nebulae visible to the naked eye from Earth.

HELPING HANDS

Often, the process of star creation is triggered by other stars. The shockwaves from a massive exploding star called a supernova (see page 20–21) can push and pull gas within a nebula to form clumps, which are the seeds of new stars.

The new stars' fierce radiation can cause the gases in the nebula around them to glow in delicate colours.

YOUNG STARS

STARS OFTEN TAKE A LONG TIME TO SETTLE DOWN AFTER THEIR BIRTH. THEY EMERGE FROM THEIR NEBULAE SURROUNDED BY CLOUDS OF GAS, WHICH THEY NEED TO GET RID OF IN ORDER TO BECOME STABLE.

OPEN CLUSTERS

Stars form in clusters that slowly drift apart over millions of years. Large groups of young stars are called 'open clusters'. They can contain dozens or even hundreds of individual stars, moving together through space, but gradually separating.

The most massive newborn stars are also the brightest and bluest. They dominate the cluster for a few million years before their fuel is exhausted. Only the more average, Sun-like stars make it out of the cluster and continue to shine for millions more years.

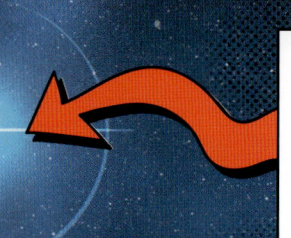

The Pleiades is one of the most well-known open clusters. It formed about 100 million years ago and is made up of about 1,000 young, blue-white stars.

GAS CLOUDS

A young star is still surrounded by a huge cloud of gas that is pulled inwards by the star's gravity. Eventually, the star will not be able to absorb any more gas. As it grows heavier, it will spin faster and faster until finally any new gas falling onto the star will be flung off again instantly.

A young star blasts unwanted gas into space. The gas is usually funnelled into jets, which shoot out from the star's poles.

It may also billow out into beautiful glowing clouds as it gets farther away from the star.

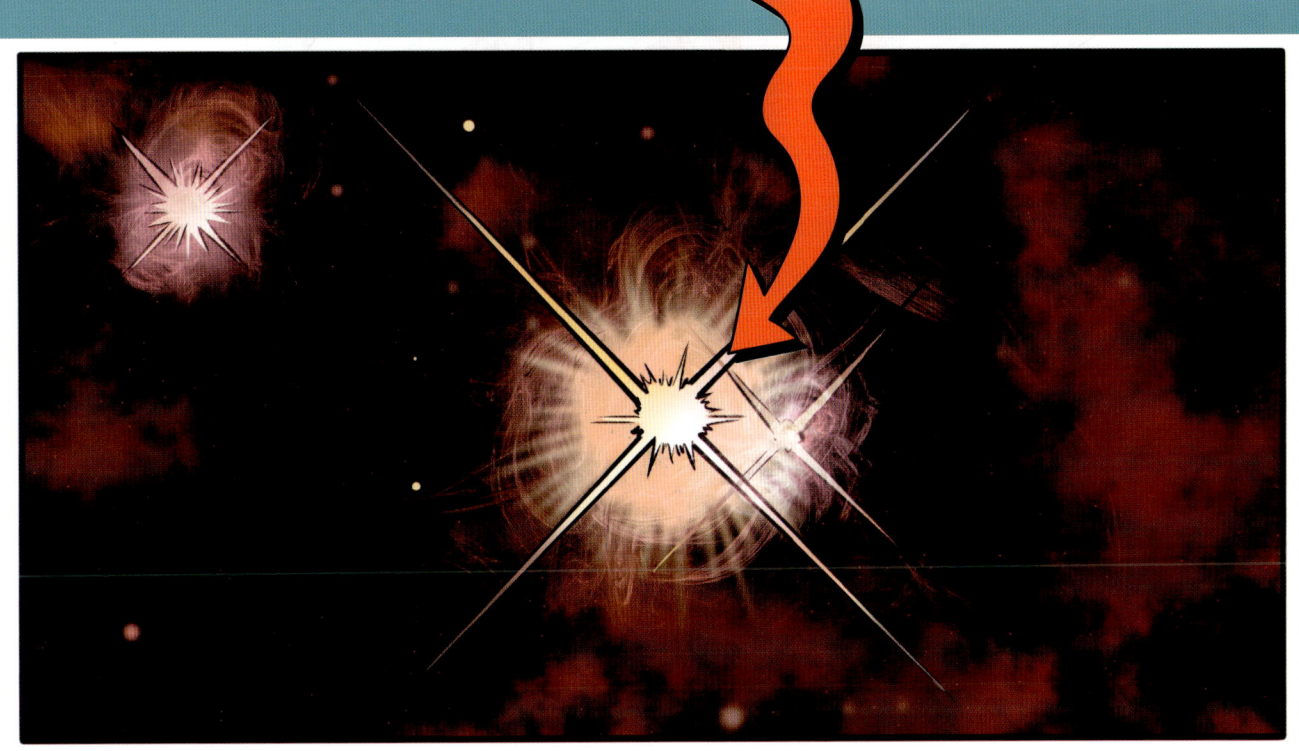

TRAVELLER'S TIPS - BUILDING SIGHTS

Watch out for solar systems under construction! As a young star settles down, it will be left with a disc of gas, ice and dust spinning around it.

Close-in to the star, only dust can survive. The dust particles collide and stick together, forming clumps that may generate enough gravity to start pulling in more material, eventually growing into rocky planets like Earth.

Farther out, gas and ice remain in huge quantities. These tend to separate into enormous orbiting fluff-balls that slowly collapse to form giant gas planets like Jupiter and Saturn.

Leftover material usually forms rocky asteroids and icy comets.

RED GIANTS

AFTER A STABLE MIDDLE AGE THAT CAN LAST FOR BILLIONS OF YEARS, A STAR WILL EVENTUALLY RUN OUT OF FUEL FOR NUCLEAR REACTIONS IN ITS CORE. AT THIS POINT, IT WILL BECOME UNSTABLE AND CHANGE ITS SIZE, BRIGHTNESS AND COLOUR, SWELLING INTO A BRILLIANT STAR CALLED A RED GIANT.

KEEP ON BURNING

When the hydrogen in a star's core is gone, the star starts to burn hydrogen in a 'shell' around the core. Eventually, the star begins to burn through the helium it has previously made, using a different type of nuclear reaction, which makes other elements including carbon and oxygen. These changes make the star unstable.

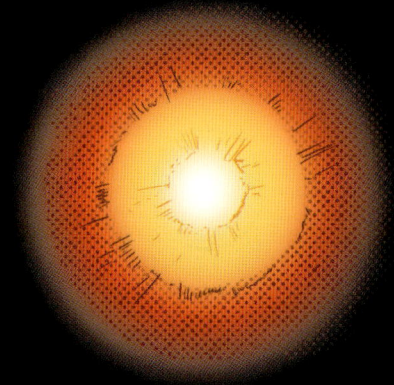

Between 300 and 400 times the diameter of our Sun, Betelgeuse is one of the brightest red giants that can be seen from Earth. The giant star has a huge hot spot twice the size of Earth's orbit in its outer shell of hydrogen gas.

TRAVELLER'S TIPS - DON'T GET FRIED!

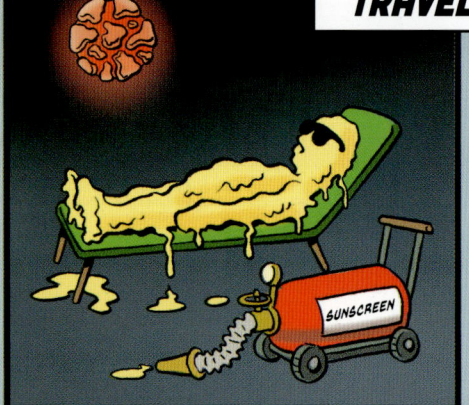

How long have we got before our Sun turns into a red giant? The lifespan of any star depends on how heavy it is, and, in this case, we're lucky that our local star is a bit of a lightweight. Our steady-burning yellow star has enough hydrogen to keep shining as it is for another 5 billion years.

Eventually, it will turn into a red giant, probably engulfing the planets Mercury and Venus and burning Earth to a crisp. If human still live on Earth in 5 billion years' time, they will have to move farther out in the solar system in order to survive.

WHY SO BIG?

Even though its main fuel supply is gone, the new type of nuclear reactions in an elderly star actually mean it gets much brighter than it was before. With more radiation pushing out, the star's upper layers billow outwards.

Eventually, a red giant can grow to hundreds of millions of kilometres across. As the star's surface gets more thinly spread, it cools down and its colour changes from yellow, blue or white to cooler orange or red.

The massive star Eta Carinae is hidden from view by the Homunculus Nebula, a debris cloud made up of two lobes produced in a violent eruption by the unstable star in the 1840s.

PLANETARY NEBULAE

MOST RED GIANTS END THEIR LIVES BY PUFFING OFF THEIR OUTER LAYERS, CREATING A GLOWING CLOUD OF EXPANDING GAS CALLED A PLANETARY NEBULA. THESE HAVE NOTHING TO DO WITH PLANETS, BUT THE RINGS OF GAS LOOK A BIT PLANET-LIKE.

THE END OF A RED GIANT

As a red giant nears the end of its life, it starts to pulsate, expanding and contracting until it expands so much that its outer layers fly off into space. Energy from the star itself keeps these cloudy nebulae shining for thousands of years. They eventually fade, and the cast-off elements in the nebula contain the raw material for making new stars.

At 700 light years away, the Helix Nebula (right) is one of the closest planetary nebulae to Earth.

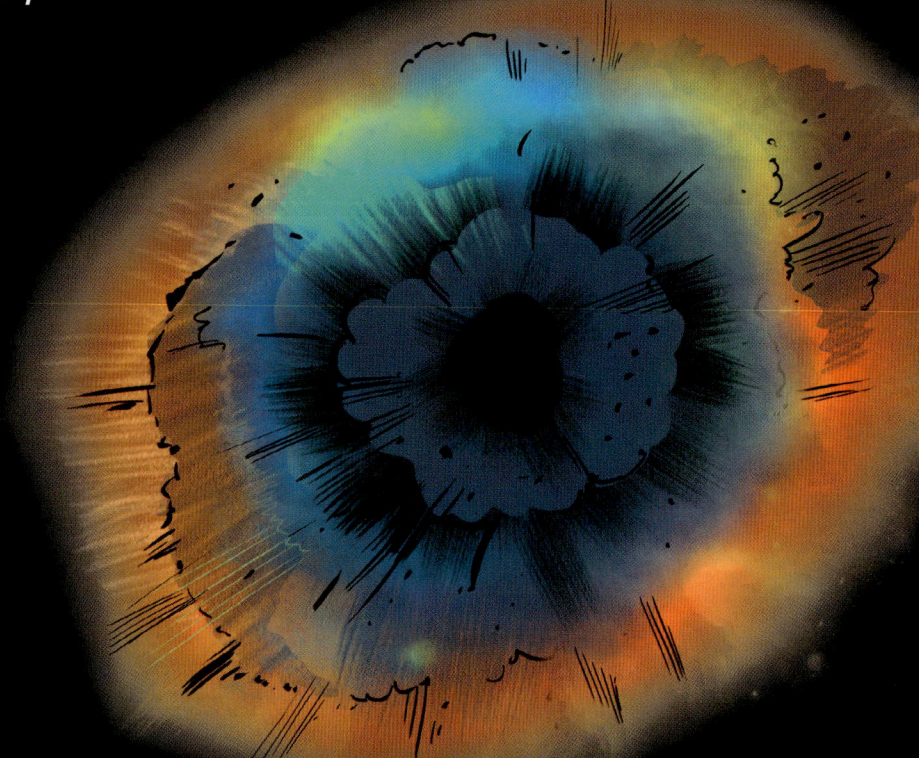

COMPLEX NEBULAE

Not all planetary nebulae form a neat spherical shell around their star. Many, such as the Cat's Eye Nebula, get twisted into amazing shapes.

One common type of complex planetary nebula has an hourglass shape – a pinch in the middle and bulges in two directions. The pinch may be caused by the presence of a smaller star, a large planet or a ring of dust orbiting close to the main star.

The Cat's Eye Nebula, with its intricate spirals of gas, is one of the most beautiful planetary nebulae.

LITTLE HEAVYWEIGHTS

As a red giant throws off its outer layers and stops producing new energy, its core – heated to millions of degrees – continues to shine. With no energy source to support it against its own weight, it slowly collapses inwards, until eventually the atoms are jammed tightly against each other, becoming a white dwarf. A tablespoon of super-dense white dwarf matter could weigh as much as a fully-grown elephant.

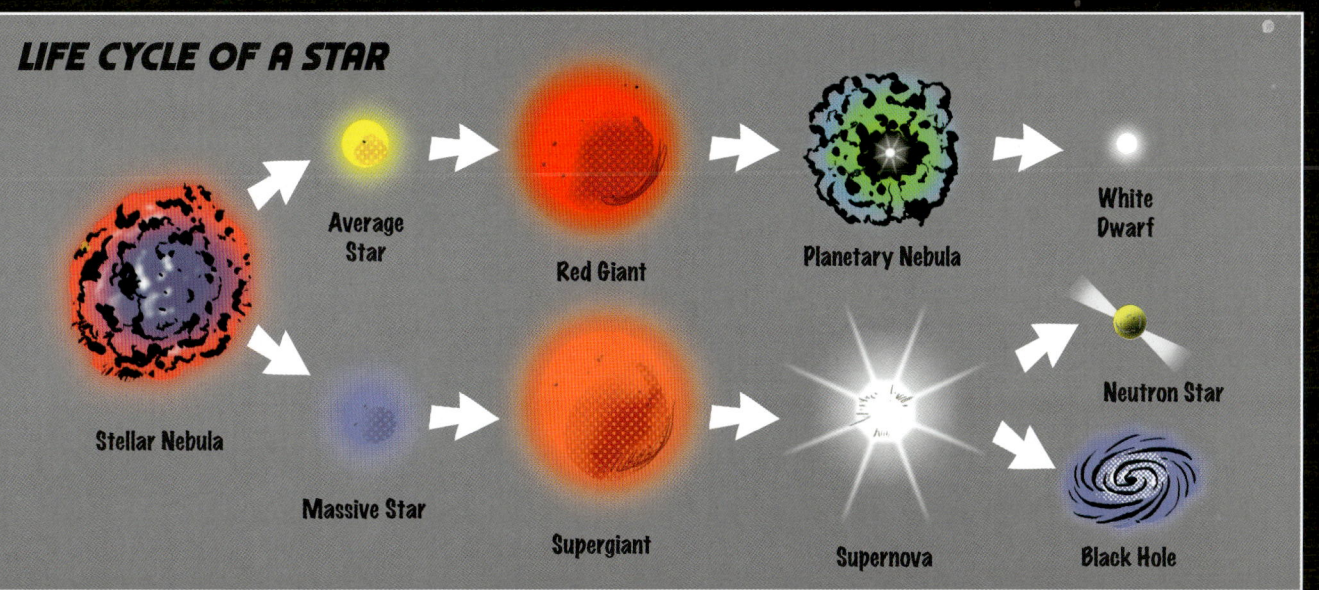

LIFE CYCLE OF A STAR

Average Star

Red Giant

Planetary Nebula

White Dwarf

Stellar Nebula

Massive Star

Supergiant

Supernova

Neutron Star

Black Hole

STARS WITH COMPANY

STARS VARY A LOT FROM ONE ANOTHER IN SIZE, WEIGHT, BRIGHTNESS AND COLOUR. MANY STARS SPEND THEIR LIVES ORBITING ONE ANOTHER IN PAIRS OR BIGGER GROUPS. SOME STARS HOLD OTHER WORLDS IN THEIR ORBITS!

DOUBLES AND MULTIPLES

Stars in pairs and groups may seem strange, but in fact our galaxy has almost as many stars in these binary and multiple systems as it does single stars like the Sun.

Stars within a group, or system, usually form at the same time and from the same chunk of nebula. The differences we often see among stars in a system help us understand how a star's mass affects its lifespan – the more massive a star is, the faster it ages.

The Trapezium is a small star cluster in the Orion Nebula. Each of the five huge, bright young stars at the heart of the Trapezium shines brighter than 10 million Suns.

SUPER-CLOSE STARS

When binary stars are very close together or very far from Earth, even the most powerful telescopes struggle to split them up. But they can still reveal themselves in other ways – either through wobbles in their light as each star pulls on the other, or through sudden dips in brightness when one star passes in front of the other and their combined light reaching Earth is reduced.

The most famous of these 'eclipsing binaries' is Algol, also called the 'Winking Demon' (see photo on page 28). Its stars are so close together that gravity from one is stealing gas from the other's outer atmosphere.

NOT TO MISS

Astronomers have detected planets orbiting thousands of distant stars. Among the best known of these alien solar systems are:

51 PEGASI: Just one planet is known to orbit this Sun-like star 50 light years from Earth. It was the first planet to be discovered around a normal star beyond our solar system.

TAU BOÖTIS: A scorching planet, far more massive than Jupiter, orbits this star every 3.3 Earth days, while a red dwarf companion star orbits much further out.

FOMALHAUT: This brilliant star is one of the brightest in the sky. It lies 25 light years from Earth and is surrounded by a ring of warm dust (see right) with a planet orbiting on its inside edge.

TRAPPIST-1: No fewer than seven planets circle this faint red dwarf star 41 light years from Earth, at distances where their surfaces could reach Earth-like temperatures.

SUPERNOVAE

NOT ALL STARS END THEIR LIVES AS PLANETARY NEBULAE AND WHITE DWARFS. RARE GIANT STARS WITH MORE THAN EIGHT TIMES THE MASS OF OUR SUN DIE IN AN EXPLOSION CALLED A SUPERNOVA, WHICH CAN BE BRIGHT ENOUGH TO OUTSHINE AN ENTIRE GALAXY!

SUPERGIANT TO SUPERNOVA

Heavyweight stars that are close to the end of their lives swell into enormous supergiants that are about ten times bigger than a normal red giant. When the fuel runs out, the star's core weighs so much that it collapses inwards in a fraction of a second. This creates a shock wave that rebounds and rips through the star's outer layers. The shock wave compresses and heats the star's outer layers so that they ignite, creating the blazing light of a supernova.

As a supergiant's core collapses, its outer layers of gases burst into a flaming supernova.

TRAVELLER'S TIPS - SOWING THE SEEDS OF LIFE

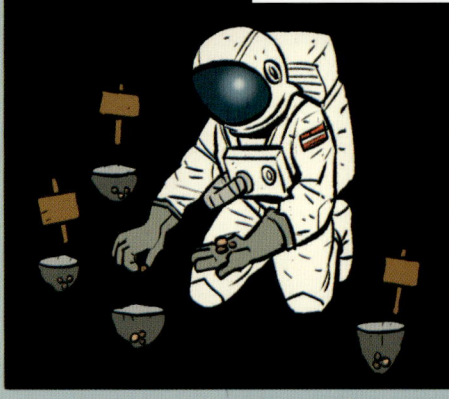

The matter blasted across space in supernova explosions is believed to be the source of all heavy elements: the rocks and metals that form a small but important part of every solid planet, including Earth. They are also a part of every living creature, including humans – we're all made up of stardust!

Matter from supernova explosions gets caught up in nebulae, where it lies waiting – often for millions of years – for the next round of star formation.

SHREDDED REMAINS

On average, one star in our galaxy goes supernova every century or so. These brilliant beacons only shine for a few weeks before fading away. However, the star's outer layers continue to expand for thousands of years as a glowing cloud called a supernova remnant.

The brightest remnant in Earth's skies is the Crab Nebula, the remains of a star that went supernova in the year 1054.

At 6,300 light years away, the sprawling Crab Nebula supernova remnant has expanded over 10 light years of space. Still heated to 18,000°C, the energy it gives out is equivalent to about 750,000 Suns.

NEUTRON STARS AND BLACK HOLES

THE CORES OF HEAVYWEIGHT STARS ARE COMPRESSED BY ENORMOUS FORCES AT THE MOMENT OF A SUPERNOVA EXPLOSION, PRODUCING SOME OF THE ODDEST OBJECTS IN THE UNIVERSE: SUPER-DENSE NEUTRON STARS AND LIGHT-GOBBLING BLACK HOLES!

NEUTRON STARS

In some massive stars, the collapse of the core is so sudden and powerful that the tiny particles that make up its atoms get jammed together to form neutrons. A neutron star may have the mass of many Suns in a space the size of an average city. It is so dense that a pinhead of matter would weigh as much as a full oil supertanker.

NOT TO MISS

Collapsed neutron stars often form an object called a pulsar. These cosmic lighthouses emit nearly all their energy in a beam that sweeps across the sky as the pulsar rotates at high speeds.

Some of the best-known pulsars include:

PSR 1919+21: The first pulsar to be discovered, in 1967. At first astronomers thought its regular radio pulses might be a signal from aliens, so they nicknamed it LGM-1 (short for 'Little Green Man')!

THE CRAB PULSAR: The pulsar, depicted below, found at the heart of the Crab Nebula (see page 21).

PSR J1748-2446AD: The fastest-spinning pulsar on record, spinning 716 times every second.

BLACK HOLES

If a star's collapsing core weighs more than about 2.2 of our Suns, its collapse will not stop at the neutron star stage. In this case, the neutrons are smashed together into even smaller particles and the core collapses to a single point in space. Gravity around the core gets so strong that, beyond a border called the event horizon, nothing can escape it – not even light, the fastest-moving thing in the Universe.

The star has become a black hole and will pull in anything that gets too close – so keep your distance!

A black hole has a dark appearance because it absorbs all the light that hits it, reflecting nothing. The collapsed star is surrounded by swirling gas and dust, drawn in by its gravity.

OUR GALAXY

OUR GALAXY, THE MILKY WAY, IS A HUGE CLOUD OF GAS, DUST AND AT LEAST 100 BILLION STARS, SPINNING IN A SPIRAL WITH A BRIGHT BULGE AT ITS CENTRE. OUR SOLAR SYSTEM LIES ROUGHLY TWO-THIRDS OF THE WAY FROM THE CENTRE TO THE OUTER EDGE, IN THE SPACE BETWEEN TWO OF THE MAJOR SPIRAL ARMS.

BAND OF STARS

When we look into space from inside the Milky Way, we can see dense star clouds forming a band across the sky. This is the galactic plane – a 'side-on' view of the Milky Way from our home inside it.

To the naked eye, stars in this band blend together to create the pale, 'milky' light that gives our galaxy its name. The clouds are brightest towards the galaxy's densely packed centre. Dark patches in the Milky Way are caused by dust clouds blocking out light.

TRAVELLER'S TIPS - THE SIZE OF THE MILKY WAY

The Milky Way is so huge that it is almost impossible to grasp its size – in fact, astronomers used to think that it made up the whole of the Universe! From edge to edge, the Milky Way is 88,000 light years across – so huge that a spacecraft travelling at about 40,000 km/h would take 2.4 billion years to cross it. Its hundreds of billions of stars are spread out so widely that they are an average of 5 light years apart.

Seen from outside, this 'overhead' view of the Milky Way shows its multi-armed spiral shape, with the arms linked to the central bulge by a short bar of stars. Astronomers believe that an enormous black hole, with an estimated mass of 4.3 million Suns, lies at the heart of the galaxy. The spiral arms are marked out by bright star-forming nebulae and short-lived clusters of stars that are constantly being replaced.

Stars circle around the galactic centre in slow orbits. Our solar system (indicated by the pointer) is a good way towards the galaxy's outer edge – our Sun takes 230 million years to complete one orbit.

OTHER GALAXIES

THE MILKY WAY IS JUST ONE GALAXY AMONG BILLIONS IN THE UNIVERSE. MOST ARE SEPARATED BY MILLIONS OF LIGHT YEARS, BUT LARGE GALAXIES SUCH AS OURS OFTEN HAVE SMALL SATELLITE GALAXIES, ORBITING LIKE MOONS AROUND A PLANET.

GALAXY TYPES

Galaxies come in a range of shapes and sizes. About a quarter are spiral galaxies, some with a bar of stars across the middle, like our Milky Way. The shape, brightness and number of spiral arms vary.

About two-thirds of known galaxies are elliptical, or ball-shaped.

These can be much bigger or smaller than spiral galaxies, and are packed with old yellow and red stars.

The rest of the known galaxies are irregular – shapeless clouds of gas and dust rich in star-birth nebulae and young blue stars.

The Pinwheel (shown left) is a swirling spiral galaxy; Fornax A (above top) has a hub but no spiral arm so is considered elliptical; Barnard's Galaxy (above bottom) is a shapeless irregular galaxy.

VIOLENT GALAXIES

Some galaxies have cores that blaze with far more light than their surrounding stars and produce huge jets blasting out into intergalactic space. These 'active galaxies' come in various types, but all have the same objects at their cores – gigantic black holes. These belch out huge amounts of energy and excess matter, heating the surrounding region.

NOT TO MISS

LARGE MAGELLANIC CLOUD: The brightest of the Milky Way's satellite galaxies, the 'LMC' is home to a vast star-birth region called the Tarantula Nebula.

ANDROMEDA GALAXY: The nearest major galaxy to our own, Andromeda is a huge spiral, 2.5 million light years away, and is just visible with the naked eye from Earth.

CIGAR GALAXY: This irregular galaxy is going through a gigantic 'starburst' – a spasm of star formation that makes it look as though the entire galaxy is exploding.

ANTENNAE GALAXIES: The spiral arms of these two galaxies have unwound as a result of a cosmic collision, while the head-on impact between their cores has triggered a huge wave of star formation.

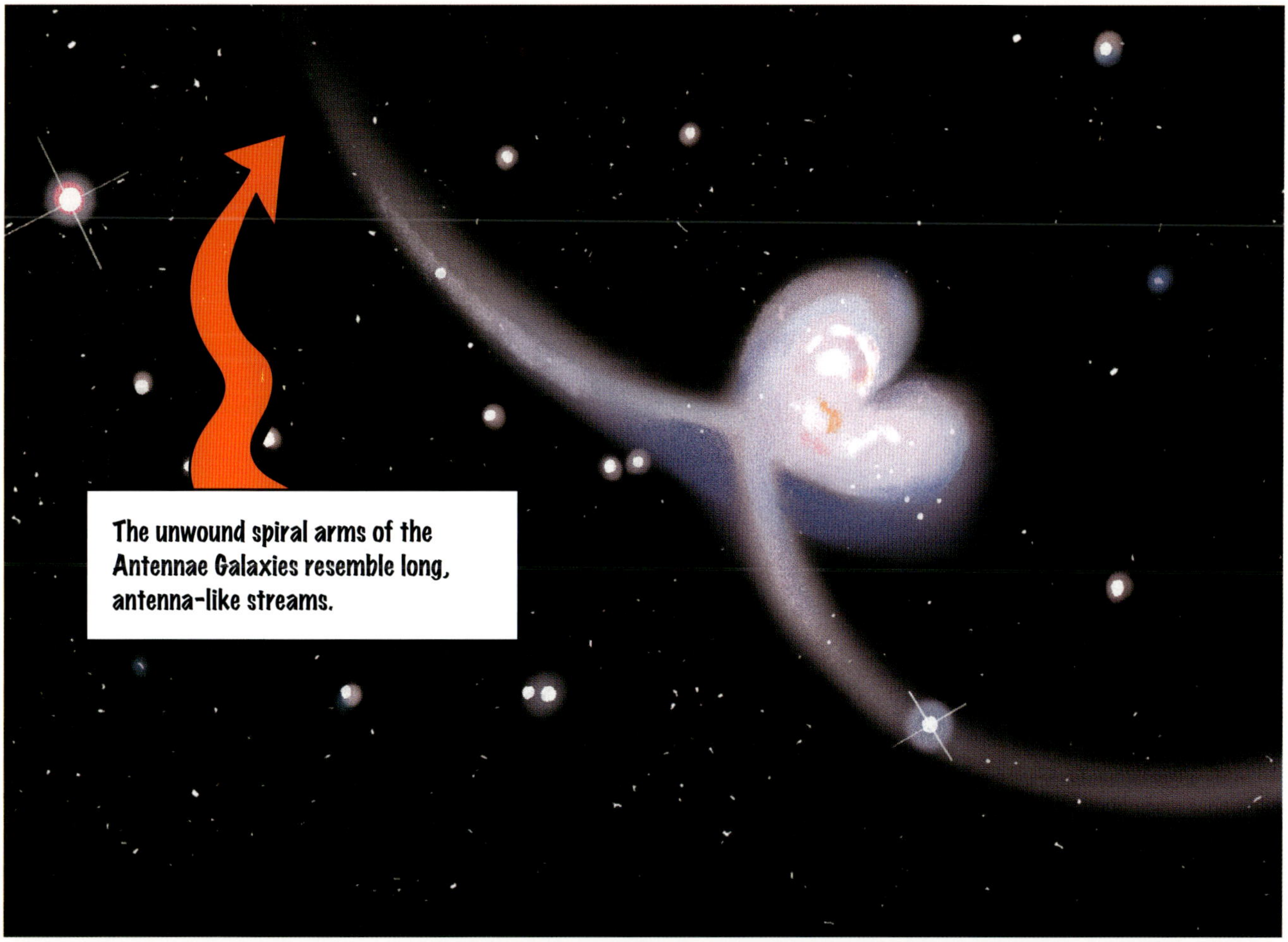

The unwound spiral arms of the Antennae Galaxies resemble long, antenna-like streams.

TOUR SNAPSHOTS

Here is a small scrapbook of photos from our trip around the Sun and stars!

The Eagle Nebula contains huge columns of gas, which are separating to form ball-shaped clumps, or globules. In time, the cores of the globules will ignite to create new stars.

The elliptical active galaxy Centaurus A recently collided with a smaller spiral galaxy. The dark dust lane across the middle shows where the spiral galaxy was absorbed.

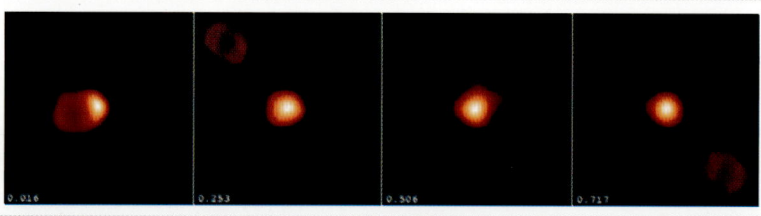

Infrared pictures of the binary star Algol, showing the movements of Algol B around the brighter Algol A.

During a solar eclipse, the Moon passes between Earth and the Sun, blocking out the star's light so the streams of hot gas that make up the Sun's outer atmosphere or corona can be seen with the naked eye.

This super-dense neutron star is known as G11.2-0.3. It is located some 16,000 light years from Earth.

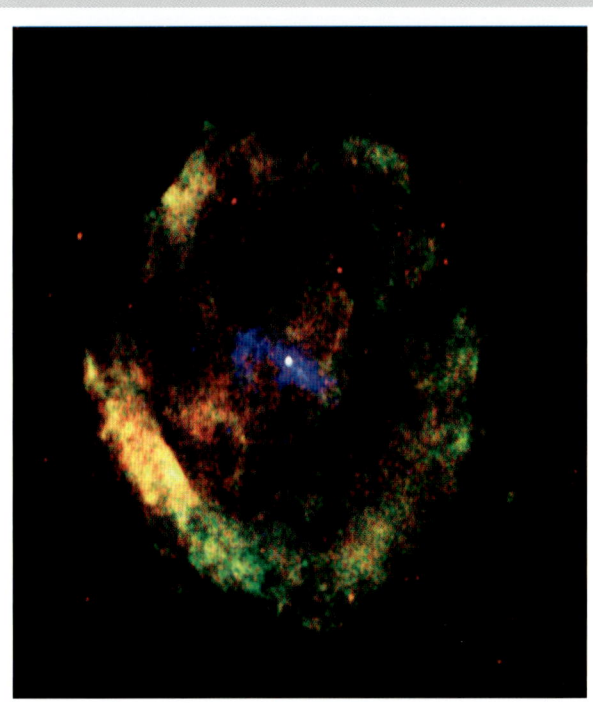

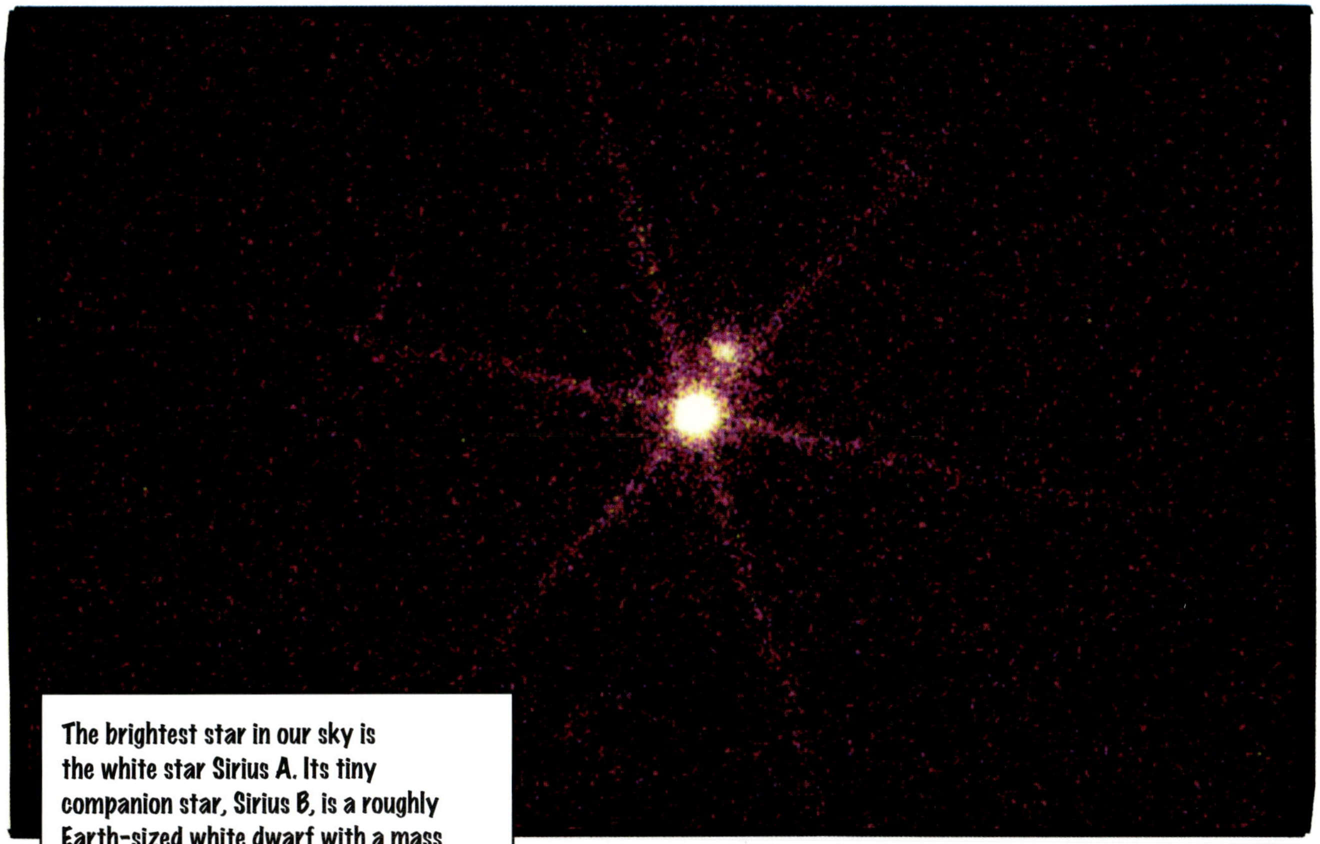

The brightest star in our sky is the white star Sirius A. Its tiny companion star, Sirius B, is a roughly Earth-sized white dwarf with a mass similar to that of the Sun.

GLOSSARY

ATMOSPHERE

A shell of gas trapped around an object by gravity.

CLUSTERS

A collection of stars or galaxies moving together through space.

CONSTELLATION

An area of the sky containing stars and other astronomical objects. Some groups of stars within a constellation may appear to form a pattern in the sky.

COSMOS

The Universe and all it contains, from planets and stars to galaxies, black holes, neutron stars and nebulae.

GALAXY

A vast number of star systems held together by gravitational attraction. Our galaxy is called the Milky Way.

GRAVITY

The force of attraction that astronomical bodies exert on each other as a result of their mass. The more massive they are, the stronger the gravitational force.

LIGHT YEAR

A unit used to measure the vast distances of space. The distance travelled by light in one year is roughly 9.5 million million kilometres.

NUCLEAR REACTION

The process in which the nucleus (core) of an atom is changed by interacting with the nucleus of another atom.

ORBIT

The curved path of one astronomical object around another as a result of gravitational attraction.

PLANET

An object that follows its own orbit around a star and is massive enough to be rounded into a spherical shape by its own gravity.

RADIATION

Energy given off by a body such as a star. A star's light is a form of radiation.

SATELLITES

Objects that orbit, or travel around, another, more massive body. Natural satellites include the moons orbiting the planets.

SOLAR SYSTEM

The family of objects in orbit around the Sun, including eight major planets and small bodies such as comets.

STAR

A huge ball of gas held together by gravity. Its core is hot and dense enough to trigger nuclear reactions that release energy, causing the star to shine.

RESOURCES

WONDERS OF THE NIGHT SKY AND
THE FUTURE OF THE UNIVERSE

By Professor Raman Prinja and Jan Bielecki, Wayland, 2022

Published in partnership with Royal Observatory Greenwich – explore space using just your eyes, and then take a leap trillions of years into the future!

RECIPE FOR A SOLAR SYSTEM

By Professor Raman Prinja and Kristina Kister, Wayland, 2023

Assemble the ingredients of our solar system as it forms over billions of years.

QUICK QUIZ

Here are three quick-fire questions to test your knowledge on the Sun and the stars.
(Answers at the bottom.) **Good luck!**

1. How big is the Sun's diameter? Is it:
   a) 1.4 million kilometres
   b) 10 million kilometres
   c) 20.5 million kilometres

2. What is a nebula made up of? Is it:
   a) planets
   b) galaxies
   c) dust and gas

3. What type of star is known as a 'cosmic lighthouse'? Is it:
   a) a red giant
   b) a pulsar
   c) a white dwarf

WEBSITES

WWW.PLANETARY.ORG/HOME
A website packed with information about the planets, the exploration of the solar system and the search for extraterrestrial intelligence.

WWW.UNIVERSETODAY.COM
Space exploration and astronomy news brought to you from around the Internet.

WWW.NASA.GOV/LEARNING-RESOURCES/
Scientists from NASA (the US National Aeronautics and Space Administration) answer your questions on the Universe.

WWW.SPACE.COM
Information on everything to do with space – satellites, stars, astronomy, the Sun, planets, NASA and more.

WWW.EDUCATION.COM/RESOURCES/OUTER-SPACE/
Interactive features and games all about outer space.

QUIZ ANSWERS: 1. A 2. C 3. B

INDEX